Ocean Life

All inquiries should be addressed to:
Barron's Educational Series, Inc.
250 Wireless Boulevard
Hauppauge, New York 11788
www.barronseduc.com

ISBN: 978-1-4380-0579-9

Library of Congress Control No. 2014935424

Date of Manufacture: January 2015
Manufactured by: Toppan Leefung Printing Co., Ltd. Dongguan, China

9 8 7 6 5 4 3 2 1

Photo credits:

Images © www.flpa-images.co.uk: laternfish, purple sea urchin © Norbert Wu/Minden Pictures/FLPA. Images © www.shutterstock.com: coral reef p14 © Richard Whitcombe; puffins © Spumador; frenzy of sharks © A Cotton Photo; humpback whales © Achimdiver; lobe-finned fish © AlessandroZocc; anemonefish © Andaman; malacca straits © anekoho; chinstrap penguins © Anton_Ivanov; coral polyp © aquapix; black skimmer © Arto Hakola; rookpool © blueeyes; triggerfish © bluehand; blue footed boobies © BlueOrange Studio; pelican diving © Brian Florky; muddy coast © BW Folsom; pelican © Catcher of Light, Inc; gannet © Charles Masters; strawberry anemones © Chelsea Cameron; wandering albatross © Christian Wilkinson; common lobster © davidpstephens; krill © digitalbalance; red sea fan © DJ Mattaar; antarctic krill © Dmytro Pylypenko; black tip shark © Dray van Beeck; whale shark © Dudarev Mikhail; jellyfish p32 © easyshutter; great white shark © Elsa Hoffmann; surfer, garibaldi © EpicStockMedia; sea nettle jellyfish, kelp air bladder, table coral, barrel sponge p16, stonefish © Ethan Daniels; anchovies, leopard shark © evantravels; cleaning shrimp © Fiona Ayerst; caribbean reef shark © frantisekhojdysz; sea lions © George Burba; high tide © GVictoria; cyclone over florida © Harvepino; manta ray © haveseen; polar bear diving © Henrik Winther Andersen; angelfish © Irina Afonskaya; adelie penguin © Jan Martin Will; horseshoe crabs © Jana Shea; humpback with open mouth © John Tunney; penguin diving © Josh Anon; blue marlin © Joshua Francis; peacock mantis shrimp © Jung Hsuan; cod fish © Krasowit; mackerel © Kristina Vackova; dolphins © Krzysztof Odziomek; egyptian seastar © LauraD; clownfish p.1 © Levent Konuk; barnacle © Lia Caldas; earth © MarcelClemens; hammerhead © Mark Doherty; tiger sharks © Matt9122; low tide © Melissa King; red rock crab © Michael Zysman; purple tube sponges © michelle peters; herring gull © nevenm; gannet colony © nickichen; sandy beach © NOBUHIRO ASADA; tube sponge © Ocean Image Photography; sea cucumber © orlandin; walrus, humpback breaching © outdoorsman; rocky coast © Patryk Kosmider; batfish with sea slater © Paul Vinten; gooseneck barnacle © Paul Yates; starfish eating sea urchin © Peter Leahy; feather star © R Gombarik; octopus © Rich Carey; orcas © Riegsecker; pacific sea nettle jellyfish © S-F; blue sea squirt © scubaluna; batwing coral crab © Sean Lema; giant clam © Sebastien Burel; great white shark © Sergey Uryadnikov; sperm whale © Shane Gross; sea lion underwater © Shin Okamoto; mandarin fish © stockpix4u; crown-of-thorns © think4photop; mouth of sea urchin, red cushion starfish © Vilainecrevette; lionfish © Vlad61; bull sharks © Willyam Bradberry; sea otter © worldswildlifewonders; king penguin © Yongyut Kumsri. Images © www.istockphoto.com: sand dollars © mardog38; starfish feet © 4kodiak; snow sign © bofotolux; sand tiger shark © StevenBenjamin. Images © National Oceanic and Atmospheric Administration (www.noaa.gov): black smoker © OAR/National Undersea Research Program (NURP); Dumbo Octopus © NOAA Okeanos Explorer Program; giant isopod © Expedition to the Deep Slope 2006, NOAA-OE; crossota © Hidden Ocean 2005 Expedition: NOAA Office of Ocean Exploration; squid larva © Matt Wilson/Jay Clark, NOAA NMFS AFSC; diatoms © NSF Polar Programs; whale blowing © NOAA; glass sponges © NOAA Okeanos Explorer Program, Gulf of Mexico 2012 Expedition.

Introduction

The oceans and seas are some of the most diverse habitats on Earth and cover about three-quarters of our planet. They help to regulate Earth's climate, produce more than half of the oxygen in the atmosphere, and absorb enormous amounts of carbon dioxide. The oceans are teeming with life, from microscopic single-celled plankton, to ferocious sharks and giant whales. These watery worlds contain some of the planet's most fascinating ecosystems.

Contents

Read on to **find** out more about **oceans** of the **world…**

The global ocean

Oceans cover about 70 percent of the **Earth's** surface, and they carry out many functions. Oceans affect the **weather** and **temperature** of our planet. They moderate Earth's temperature by absorbing heat from the **Sun**. The ocean's waves and **currents** distribute this heat energy around the world, heating the land and air during winter and **cooling** them during summer. There are five **oceans** on Earth, and they are all connected to one another. **Seas** are smaller than oceans, but far more numerous. Most seas are bordered in part or **completely** by land.

Facts and figures

The oceans of the world

Pacific Ocean
The largest ocean, covering about 30 percent of the Earth's surface. The word "pacific" means "peaceful."

Atlantic Ocean
The second largest ocean is the Atlantic, and it covers 21 percent of the planet. It separates the American continents from Europe and Africa.

Indian Ocean
The third largest ocean covers 14 percent of the planet. It lies between Africa and Australasia.

Southern Ocean
This ocean covers about 4 percent of the Earth's surface. It has powerful winds and currents and icebergs.

Arctic Ocean
This is the smallest and shallowest ocean. It is mostly covered by sea ice during winter.

Deepest point

The Mariana Trench in the Pacific Ocean is the deepest place on Earth. It is 6.8 miles in depth.

Salt and fresh water

Barely 3 percent of water on Earth is fresh; 97.5 percent is salty. Two percent of freshwater is frozen in glaciers. The rest, in lakes and rivers, is drinking water.

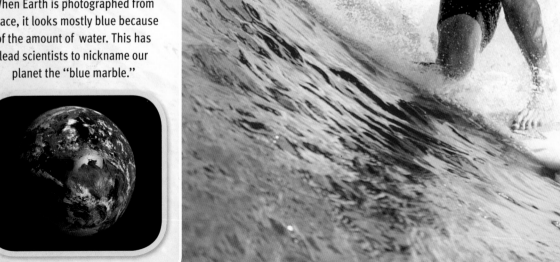

A surfer riding a large wave off the coast of Hawaii

Did you know?

When Earth is photographed from space, it looks mostly blue because of the amount of water. This has lead scientists to nickname our planet the "blue marble."

High tide at Hopewell Rocks, in Canada

Low tide at Hopewell Rocks, in Canada

Water levels

Every 12 hours or so, seawater rises and recedes. These movements are called tides. As Earth turns, the Moon "pulls" the seawater toward itself, causing water to rise. High and low tides are most noticeable along coasts, where rocks and beaches are exposed and then submerged under water.

Ocean storms

Enormous tropical storms with powerful winds and heavy rain can develop over warm waters. These storms, called hurricanes, can be hundreds of miles across. Hurricanes also create tornadoes, high waves, and widespread flooding when they hit land, causing devastation.

A hurricane near the coast of Florida

Some of the largest waves can be found around the Hawaiian Islands in the Pacific Ocean.

Ocean study

Scientists who study marine ecosystems, ocean circulation, and geology are called oceanographers.

Salty water

As rainwater flows over and under land on its way to the sea, it collects mineral salts. As seawater evaporates, the saltiness increases.

Ocean highways

As the modern world developed, many countries began trading goods with each other. Soon sea routes were established and ships began carrying goods from continent to continent. Hundreds of years later we still use the oceans to transport commodities, foods, and fuels around the world.

Ships on the Strait of Malacca, Malaysia

Down through the zones

An ocean can be divided into layers, or **zones**. Each zone is defined by the amount of **sunlight** it receives, its depth, and its level of water **pressure**. The top zone, called the sunlight zone, receives the most sunlight, and it is here that **aquatic** plants are able to grow. As you travel **down** through the twilight zone and into the midnight zone, it becomes colder and **darker**, oxygen levels are reduced, and pressure increases with the **weight** of the water above. Some sea **creatures** live their whole lives in a single zone, while others have to move **between** zones in order to survive.

Facts and figures

Oceanic zones

Sunlight zone
Surface–650 feet
This zone gets lots of light and the Sun warms the water. Animal and plant life are plentiful.

Twilight zone
650–3,300 feet
Little light reaches this zone, so the water is cooler. Water pressure is increasing. Creatures that produce light start to appear in this zone.

Midnight zone
3,300–13,000 feet
Animals that live in this cold, dark zone are often black or red in color due to lack of sunlight.

The Abyss
13,000–20,000 feet
There is no light and it is near freezing.

The Trenches
20,000–36,000 feet
Almost freezing water, and with water pressure equal to the weight of eight 747 aircraft.

Did you know?

The lanternfish is bioluminescent, producing light by a chemical reaction in its photophores. At night it migrates from the twilight zone to the surface to feed on plankton.

Almost unknown

Humans have only explored about 5 percent of the oceans. In fact, we have better maps of Mars than of the ocean floor!

Undersea mountains

The mid-ocean ridges make up Earth's longest mountain range. It is 40,000 miles long, and 90 percent of it is underwater. It circles the globe like the seam on a tennis ball.

Teams of dolphins herd sardines into a densely packed shoal near the surface of the water

Over 90 percent of all marine life lives in the sunlight zone.

A sperm whale beginning its dive

Odd and odder

Animals that live in the midnight zone are some of the oddest creatures on Earth. They have adapted to life in a dark, cold world where food is scarce.

Crossota

This blood-red jellyfish is found in all oceans. Its bell-shaped body grows to a size of an inch and has 275 tentacles.

Dumbo octopus

This mollusc gets its name from two earlike fins that resemble elephant ears. Its tentacles spread out like a skirt when it swims.

Giant isopod

This crustacean is related to the wood louse, and one species measured 30 inches. It can go for long periods without food.

Deep diver

The sperm whale can swim into the midnight zone. Before diving, it exhales all the air from its lungs to help it survive the intense water pressure. Scientists believe that whales swim upside down so they can see prey against the lighter water above, and then they attack from below!

Black smokers

Chimneys, called black smokers, expel hot fluid and are typically found on the floor of the abyss. They are powered by water below the Earth's crust and create a unique environment where creatures, such as giant tubeworms, have adapted to survive the extreme pressure and the dark.

A black smoker expelling hot water

Sunlight hunter

The blue marlin is an apex predator, meaning it has no natural predators within its ecosystem. This large fish hunts for its food in the sunlight zone. It will approach a school of fish at full speed, slashing through them with its daggerlike bill. It then returns to consume the stunned or dead prey.

A blue marlin at the water's surface

Marine food chains

Each **ecosystem** has its own food chain that shows the feeding connections between **species**. On the lowest level of the chain are **plankton**, which includes phytoplankton and zooplankton. The next level contains the **herbivores** who eat the phytoplankton and incorporate this energy into their own **tissues**. The **highest** levels contain animals—some that are microscopic and some that are ocean giants and apex **predators**—which eat other **organisms** for energy. If a link in the food chain breaks, it **threatens** the survival of all organisms in the chain.

Facts and figures

The food chain

The Sun
The Sun provides the energy for a food chain.

The producers
They use the Sun's energy to make food to store in their tissues.

The consumers
Consumers cannot make their own energy but get it by eating the producers or consumers below them in the food chain. There are five levels of consumers.

Herbivore consumers
The lowest consumers, like krill and mussels, eat the producers.

Level 1 consumers
These carnivores eat herbivore consumers.

Levels 2–3 consumers
Larger carnivorous animals eat 1st and 2nd level consumers.

Levels 4–5 consumers
These consumers, such as sharks and whales, have no predators.

Mackerel eat small crustaceans and fish. They are eaten by larger animals including tuna, sharks and pelicans.

Did you know?

A pelican catches its food by scooping fish into its pouched bill. It squeezes the water from the pouch, tilts back its head, and swallows the fish whole.

Threat of overfishing

A great threat to the marine food chain is overfishing by humans. Taking too many fish from a habitat can destroy the physical environment and distort the entire food chain.

Sea garden

Seaweeds are algae and are producers in the food chain. They need seawater, sunlight, and an attachment point in order to grow.

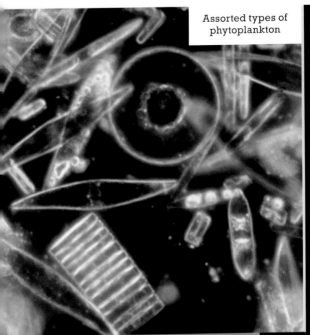

Assorted types of phytoplankton

Octopus larvae are a type of zooplankton

Microorganism

Plankton is the most basic organism in the ocean and is crucial in the food chain. There are two types of plankton, microscopic plants called phytoplankton and weak-swimming tiny animals called zooplankton. Some zooplankton is made of baby animals that will grow into strong-swimming, non-planktonic adults.

Drifting jellyfish

Jellyfish primarily eat plankton, but larger specimens will also eat small crustaceans and fish. Some species are cannibalistic and will feed on other jellyfish. They use their stinging tentacles to catch their prey. Many species of sea turtle feed on jellyfish.

A group of Pacific sea nettle jellyfish

Flying predators

Sea birds, such as albatross, eat aquatic animals, so they have an important role in the food chain.

Endless chain

Decomposers, such as marine worms, break down organic waste and dead plants and animals. These nutrients then re-enter the food chain.

Rising ocean temperatures are reducing phytoplankton numbers by one percent every year.

Top predator

The great white shark is at the top of the marine food chain. It uses five senses—smell, taste, touch, sight, and hearing—to capture prey, but is also able to sense electric fields through its pores. The shark uses this to navigate the oceans following a map of Earth's magnetic fields.

A great white shark catching a seal

Coastal life

Coastlines are areas where land meets an **ocean** or other large body of water. These areas are full of life, with plants, **algae**, flowers, **fish**, crustaceans, aquatic mammals, and insects all making their homes here. **Rock pools** are formed at low tide. They provide **shelter** for many creatures that live below the waves. Cliff tops along coastal areas are important **nesting** places for many **seabirds**. Coastal habitats also serve a vital function in the marine food chain and wider **environment**, providing feeding, **spawning**, and nursery areas for many species.

Did you know?

Manmade harbors and ports are classed as areas of coastline. A large group of sea lions has relocated from rocky islands outside San Francisco Bay to wooden piers inside the bay.

Low tide along the coastline of Washington

Coral sand

Parrotfish eat coral, which is broken down and emerges from them as grains of sand. A parrotfish can produce 220 pounds of beautiful, fine, white coral beach sand a year!

Working together

Colorful lichens often cover the rocks on coastlines. They are created when a fungi and algae grow together.

The **rapidly changing** conditions of a rock pool make survival a challenge.

A large cluster of blue mussels

Mussel power

Blue mussels are bivalve molluscs. This means they are simple animals with a soft body, protected by a hard shell that has two hinged parts. Mussels can be found on exposed shores, where they attach themselves with strong threads to rocks. They feed on plankton and other microscopic creatures.

Ancient crab

Horseshoe crabs are not true crabs as their name suggests, but are closely related to spiders, ticks, and scorpions. Horseshoe crabs are primitive animals that have existed in their present form for over 360 million years. They live in deep water, but come ashore once a year to mate.

On the cliffs

Puffins spend most of their lives at sea, but in the spring they return to the cliffs where they hatched. Here they form colonies of up to one million nests. Pairs of puffins will nest between rocks and under boulders. If there is soil, they will make a nesting burrow or move into an empty rabbit burrow.

Atlantic horseshoe crabs on the shore

Atlantic puffins on a rocky cliff

Ocean forests

In the oceans and seas there are forests and **meadows** of seaweeds and **seagrasses**. Just like forests on land, these unusual **ecosystems** are bursting with life as they provide food and shelter for many species of animals. These watery **forests** and meadows help protect **coastlines** by absorbing the wave energy caused by **hurricanes** and storms. In addition, these ecosystems are highly efficient at extracting **damaging** carbon dioxide out of the **environment**, meaning that they play an important role in combating **global** warming.

Seagrasses and seaweeds provide hiding places, breeding grounds and protective nurseries.

A large Pacific sea nettle jellyfish at the edge of a Californian kelp forest

Seagrass origins

Unlike seaweeds that originated in the oceans, seagrasses came from flowering plants that grew on dry land.

A useful plant

Kelp are large seaweeds. They are used in the manufacture of toothpastes, shampoos, salad dressings, puddings and cakes, dairy products, frozen foods, medicines, and more!

Did you know?

Sea otters find their favorite food, sea urchins, in and around kelp forests. The otters wrap kelp stems around their bodies to stop them drifting away on the current while resting and eating.

Gassy floats

Like plants on dry land, kelp grows by using the Sun, through the process of photosynthesis, to produce energy. Kelp plants have floats, called bladders, which are small gas-filled balloons at the base of their blades. The bladders help the blades float so that they can absorb maximum sunlight.

Air bladders on a giant kelp plant

An octopus hunting in a seagrass meadow

Grassy meadows

Seagrasses are found in tropical and colder regions. Like grasses on land, they form large meadows, produce flowers and seeds, and are home to a diverse number of organisms. One seagrass plant can give rise to many stems, which are all connected by underground roots over a wide area.

Hungry urchins

Sea urchins are the number one enemy of seaweed forests. These tiny, colorful creatures feed on the shoots and leaves of the plant and can demolish large areas of these underwater habitats. Starfish, ocean catfish, and otters eat sea urchins, and in doing so help to control urchin numbers.

Purple sea urchins eating seaweed

Coral reefs

Coral reefs are underwater structures made of the **skeletons** of coral, which are marine invertebrate **animals**. These reefs are found in warm, shallow waters around the **Equator**. Reefs are the **oldest** ecosystems and support more species per foot than any other environment. They protect **coastlines** against wave damage caused by **hurricanes** and storms. They provide the sand on beautiful coral beaches. Reefs are feeding, **spawning**, and nursery **habitats** for many ocean creatures and provide food and livelihoods for about one **billion** people worldwide.

Coral gets its colors from the tiny algae that live in it

Facts and figures

Largest barrier reef
The Great Barrier Reef, off the Australian coast, stretches for 1,400 miles.

Most diverse reef
The Coral Triangle is a huge expanse of reefs lying in waters between Indonesia, Malaysia, Papua New Guinea, Philippines, Solomon Islands, and Timor. It contains 75 percent of all known coral species and 3,000 fish species.

Fastest-growing coral
Staghorn corals can grow 6 inches a year.

Rarest coral
Thought extinct since the 1890s, a colony of elkhorn coral has been found off the Marshall Islands in the northern Pacific Ocean.

Oldest coral colony
A black coral, collected off Hawaii, has been carbon-dated as being 4,265 years old.

Reefs are home to 15 percent of known fish species but cover less than one percent of the world.

Did you know?

A coral polyp is only 1–3 millimeters across and grows 10 millimeters a year. Polyps can colonize huge tracts of seabed, but it takes about 300,000 years for a reef to form.

New species

Scientists and researchers believe that there are still millions of new species to be discovered living on the world's coral reefs.

Under threat

One-fifth of the planet's reefs are so seriously damaged they are beyond recovery. Of the remaining reefs, about half could die unless coral starts to regrow.

Hard coral: 10-foot table corals

Soft coral: red sea fan moving in the current

Reef fish
The reefs are home to about 4,000 species of fish. These fish are among the most colorful and beautifully patterned of any creature in the oceans.

Emperor angelfish
The dark stripe across its eyes is meant to confuse predators—they are unable to tell if the angelfish is approaching.

Hard and soft

There are 800 species of hard coral. The polyps have clusters of six tentacles. Algae in the polyp's tissue provide the materials to make the hard calcium carbonate skeleton. Soft coral polyps have eight tentacles and most have no hard "skeleton." They move in the current and have a jellylike feel.

Giant clam

Giant clams fix themselves to coral reefs and stay there for their whole lives. They are the largest molluscs on Earth and achieve their enormous size by consuming the sugars and proteins produced by the billions of algae that live in their tissues.

The giant clam, like coral, relies on algae

Clown triggerfish
To avoid being preyed upon, this fish can extend its fins to lock itself into crevices. It uncovers its own food by squirting water at it.

Cleaner shrimp

Cleaner shrimps are found on many coral reefs. They benefit from a symbiotic relationship. In return for cleaning larger sea creatures, the shrimp gets its fill of nutritious parasites from the host's body. Up to 25 shrimps will congregate at "cleaning stations" and do a dance to attract a host.

Pacific cleaner shrimp at work

Mandarinfish
Named for its coloring, which resembles the robes of a Chinese mandarin, its skin releases toxins to warn predators to back off.

Other plantlike animals

When it comes to **peculiar** animals, these are perhaps the **oddest** of all. The green sea slug is an animal that behaves like a plant, while the sea anemone looks like a **flower** but is, in fact, a predatory animal. These **mostly** immobile animals are **filter** feeders that strain plankton and algae from the water. Though all are found in shallow **tropical** water—often coral reefs—some are at home in cold water at great **depths**. These plantlike animals are found **attached** to rocks or wrecks and sometimes **embedded** in sand, living alone or in communities.

Some of the largest sponges may be over 100 years old.

Small fish and many invertebrates live on and in this huge barrel sponge

Easy being green

The green sea slug is able to extract photosynthesizing genes from the algae it eats. The slug then uses this to make chlorophyll, in the same way as a plant!

Snail fur

Snail fur is a tiny plantlike animal that colonizes the shell of a hermit crab. If its head is cut off, snail fur will grow another in a few days.

Did you know?

Sea squirts are a favored food in South Korea, where they are known as sea pineapples. They are often eaten raw or pickled. Sea squirts are also food for colorful sea slugs!

A clever fish

Frogfish, or anglerfish, are irregularly shaped with bumpy, scaleless skin that is colored to perfectly mimic sponges, like the purple tube sponge. Frogfish hide among the sponges to avoid getting eaten, while at the same time waiting for their own unsuspecting prey to approach.

Living together

Anemonefish are immune to anemone toxin and hide in the anemone's tentacles and graze on leftover food. In return, the anemonefish shoos away predators and removes parasites. Anemones will sometimes attach themselves to hermit crabs—the camouflage protects the crab.

A frogfish hides among tube sponges

Some anemonefish and their host

Plant mimics

Fixed to rocks and reefs with flowerlike heads and bodies like tree trunks, it is easy to think that these animals are plants.

Sponges

Found at all depths and in all waters, sponges have changed little in 600 million years. They help keep water clean and clear.

Sea anemone

It eats and expels waste through a single orifice surrounded by stinging tentacles. It feeds on plankton and small fish.

Sea squirts

Often found on piers and boat hulls, they have separate openings for food and waste. They squirt a jet of water when agitated.

Filter feeders

These animals filter their food—bacteria, plankton, and small animals—from the water. Glass sponges are filter feeders. Silica needles fuse together to make their netlike skeletons, and when water passes through the net, food is extracted. The net will also trap small animals.

Venus flower glass sponges with a squat lobster in the middle

Icy waters

The Southern and Arctic oceans are **different** from other oceans on Earth. They are **colder**, so the water is denser and sea ice and icebergs increase the **saltiness** of the water. As the denser water sinks, surface water is pulled in, creating huge **circulating** currents **thousands** of feet below the oceans' surface. The **Southern** Ocean surrounds the Antarctic land mass, while the **Arctic** Ocean has no land masses at all. Scientists believe that polar marine creatures have fewer offspring, live **longer**, and grow larger, though more **slowly** than their warmer-water relatives.

Facts and figures

Fastest penguin swim
Gentoo penguins have been timed at 22 miles per hour!

Largest penguin colony
Two million chinstrap penguins gather to breed on Zavodovski Island, in the southern Atlantic Ocean.

Longest migration
Adelie penguins cover 8,000 miles a year between summer breeding sites and their winter hunting grounds.

Biggest seal
The record is held by a southern elephant bull seal that weighed 11,000 pounds and measured 22 1/2 feet.

Most numerous
There are almost 12 million mating pairs of macaroni penguins in the world. This is a penguin record!

Fiercest polar animals
The polar bear and the Greenland shark share this honor.

Did you know?

Krill, a shrimplike crustacean, is the favorite food of the planet's largest animal, the blue whale. Krill eat the phytoplankton that thrive in the Southern Ocean.

A polar bear swimming in the icy water of the Arctic Ocean

Giant shark

The Greenland shark, found in waters 2,000 feet deep under the Arctic ice, can grow to 26 feet and can kill a polar bear, though its normal diet is seal.

Polar dip

The polar bear paddles with its front paws and steers with its hind paws. It has a layer of warming blubber, and its nostrils close underwater.

Polar bears can SWIM for days at a time and cover hundreds of miles.

A herd of walruses resting on the Arctic sea ice

Southern penguins

These flightless birds spend most of their life in water. They catch krill, fish, and squid in their beaks and swallow them whole.

Chinstrap penguin

Found on the Antarctic Peninsula and islands of the South Atlantic, its colonies can consist of 100,000 breeding pairs.

Mighty walrus

A walrus spends a third of its life on sea ice and prefers snow-covered moving pack ice or ice flows to land. A layer of blubber, up to 6 inches thick, keeps it warm. It eats tubeworms, corals, crabs, shrimps, bivalve molluscs, seals, and even other walruses. Killer whales and humans are its predators.

A weddell seal below a breathing hole in the Antarctic Ocean

Adélie penguin

It spends summer on the Antarctic coasts. In winter it lives on pack ice that is thousands of miles from its summer home.

A perfect home

Some species of seal depend on sea ice to survive. It provides them with a frozen shelter in which to raise their cubs. Some seals use their teeth to keep natural holes in the ice open. They will use these "breathing holes" to enter and exit the water while hunting and to escape predators.

"Spyhopping"

Spyhopping is a special behavior among whales and dolphins. They leap from the water, then bob about with their heads above the water so they can have a look around. To hold this position, they kick their tail flukes. It is similar to humans treading water.

King penguin

Found on many islands in the Southern Ocean, it never ventures onto pack ice. It incubates its egg on the top of its feet.

Arctic killer whales "spyhopping"

Giants of the ocean

Whales are warm-blooded **mammals** that can be found in all oceans, but each species will have its own **range** and migration routes. Whales are intelligent, **social** animals that nurture their young and **communicate** using movement, clicks, and songs. They live together in **pods** of between 2 and 40 whales, except for blue and gray whales, which are **solitary**. Whales have shown that, **within** the pod, they cooperate, plan, teach, and even **grieve**. A lot is known about these magnificent animals, but there is much, much more to discover and **understand**.

Facts and figures

Largest whale
The record is held by a blue whale that measured 108 feet. Its heart was the size of a small car.

Longest life span
The bowhead whale is thought to be one of Earth's longest living animals, with a life span of 177–245 years.

Deepest diver
Cuvier's beaked whale can dive to depths of 9,800 feet.

Longest migration
A female humpback travelled 6,000 miles from Brazil in South America to Madagascar, off the east coast of Africa.

Most endangered
Northern right whales and blue whales are endangered. The North Pacific northern right whale is nearly extinct.

Smallest whale
The dwarf sperm whale measures 10 feet.

Humpback whales travel in pods of up to 15 members

Did you know?

Some whales have teeth, others have baleen plates, that are covered with hairs that filter food from the water. The blue, fin, and humpback are examples of baleen whales.

Long distance

The gray whale can travel 12,400 miles in its migration from summer feeding waters to winter breeding grounds.

Top of the chain

Whales are at the apex of the food chain, meaning they have few predators. But these giants are in trouble, with 7 of the 13 great whale species regarded as vulnerable or endangered.

A humpback leaping clear of the water

A big leap!

Humpback whales are not only famous for their extra-long flippers, humped back, and mating songs, but also for their athleticism. They can use their flippers and tail to propel themselves clear of the water! That takes some power when you consider they can weigh more than 40 small cars!

Mother and calf

After a long gestation, mother and calf form a strong bond, often staying virtually side by side—and even resting on its mother's head—for the first six months. After that the young calf will go on short forays alone, but will continue to feed on its mother's milk for a year or more.

Whale song

Humpback whales communicate, especially when migrating or mating, by singing. The songs may last for 30 minutes.

Clever!

A whale navigates using echolocation. Tissues in the whale's head process a reflected sound (an echo) so it can map its surroundings.

The **blue whale** is the **loudest animal** on **Earth.** Its call measures **188** decibels, **louder** than a jet engine!

A female pilot whale with calves

There she blows!

Baleen whales have two blowholes; toothed whales one. Whales can dive to great depths, but have to come to the surface to breathe. Blowholes, which are sealed under water, open at the surface to exhale air and mucus and to inhale fresh air. A vapor spout can reach 30 feet into the air.

Endangered right whale spouting

Fish

Marine **ecosystems** and the fish that inhabit them have a very **complex** relationship, and one that is jeopardized by commercial fishing, pollution, and a changing environment. The **diversity** of fish is **astounding**—from tiny, colorful fish that dart in and out of corals to deep-sea **monsters**, such as the Atlantic wolffish; from timid angelfish to **sleek** hunting machines, such as sharks and marlin. Although **different** from each other, they are all closely **connected** by the marine food chain, with even fish excreta being recycled as a **fertilizer** for algae and seagrasses.

Facts and figures

Top predator
The great white shark is the prime predator of marine fish and birds. It is also responsible for many attacks on humans.

Fastest swimmer
The sailfish can swim short distances at 68 miles per hour.

Largest school
It has been estimated that North Atlantic herring schools contain about three billion fish!

Most toxic fish to eat
The pufferfish is served as the delicacy fugu in restaurants in Japan. If it is not correctly prepared, its toxin, which is 1,200 times stronger than cyanide, can be lethal.

Deepest, darkest home
The hadal snailfish has been recorded living in water down to a depth of 4.7 miles—where the water is near-freezing and it is completely dark!

Bony fish

The red lionfish (right) clearly shows the bony spines that connect the fins to its body. The showy fins are venomous and can easily puncture skin. When disturbed, it flares its fins before attacking.

A red lionfish swimming over a coral reef in the Red Sea, Egypt

Over-fishing

In 2012, commercial fishing extracted 90 million tons of fish from the seas. Overfishing is a global problem.

Did you know?

The ocean sunfish is the heaviest bony fish in the world, weighing in at 2,200 pounds. It has a fish's head and tail, with no body in the middle. It eats an awful lot of jellyfish!

After a 10-year study, scientists reported that there are 16,764 species of marine fish.

An anchovy with mouth and gills open

Breathing in water

Fish breathe oxygen that is dissolved in the water. As fish swim, water enters the open mouth and flows over layers of feathery gills in the throat. In the gills, oxygen is extracted from the water and enters the fish's bloodstream. The gills pass carbon dioxide from the bloodstream into the water.

Fact file

Types of fish

Fish make up the largest group of vertebrates—animals with a backbone and spinal column. There are four main types of fish.

Jawless fish
Lampreys and hagfish are fish without jaws. Their smooth, eel-shaped bodies have no scales.

Fish with cartilage
This includes sharks, rays, skates, and chimaeras that all have skeletons made of cartilage, not bone.

Fatal stings

Ugly and dangerous are two words for the stonefish. Its dorsal spines can deliver fatal stings to humans. Camouflaged to look like an encrusted rock or piece of coral, the stonefish lies completely still until its prey swims by. It then takes and consumes its meal with amazing speed.

A deadly stonefish lies in wait

Giant fish

The manta ray can grow to 26 feet with fins measuring 23 feet, tip to tip. It is a giant fish, but it is dwarfed by the whale shark, coming in at around 39–46 feet. Though large, both of these fish feed on plankton. To filter as much water as possible, their mouths open very wide.

Lobe-finned fish
These ancient fish have limblike fins that move in an alternating pattern, like the legs of a trotting horse.

Ray-finned fish
This is the largest group, incorporating all bony fish that have fins attached to the body with bony spines.

Manta ray: mouth open and feeding

Sharks

There are more than **465** species of shark, but only a handful of them have become **infamous**. There are 8 categories of shark: flattened **angel** sharks, saw sharks, dogfish sharks, large-jawed mackerel sharks, placid carpet sharks, **bullhead** sharks, frilled and cow sharks, and **ground** sharks, which include some of the most **feared** hunters. Sharks live in all oceans around the world, and some **roam** far and wide. Most sharks produce only a few young, but within hours of being born, the **pups**, which have a full set of **teeth**, swim off and are ready to feed and fend for themselves.

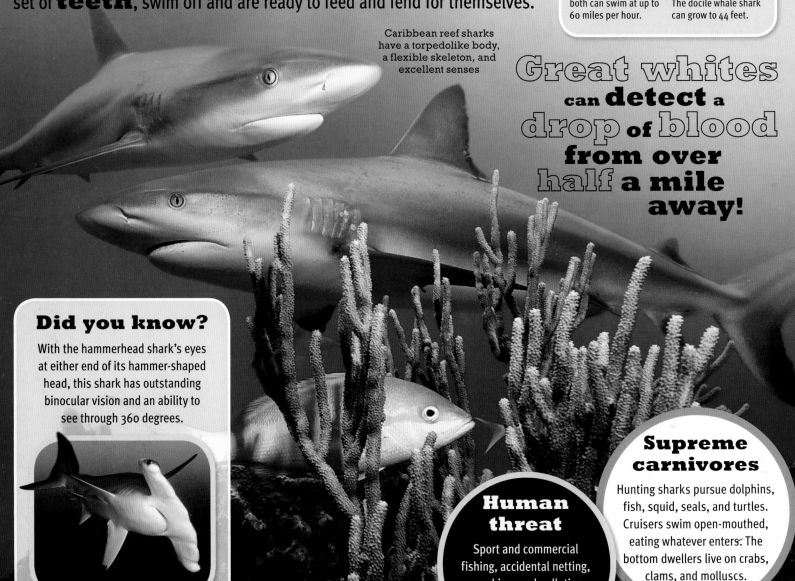

Caribbean reef sharks have a torpedolike body, a flexible skeleton, and excellent senses

Facts and figures

Smallest shark
At just 6 inches, you could hold the dwarf lantern shark in your hands. Rarely seen, it lives at depths below 820 feet.

How many teeth?
Over the course of its life, a shark could grow over 20,000 teeth.

Fastest sharks
It is a tie between mako sharks and blue sharks: both can swim at up to 60 miles per hour.

Long-range hunter
A great white shark was recorded swimming 12,427 miles between South Africa and Australia.

Fresh and salt water
The bull shark can tolerate both fresh and salt water. It has been found 2,500 miles up the Amazon River in South America.

Largest shark
The docile whale shark can grow to 44 feet.

Great whites can **detect a drop of blood from over half a mile away!**

Did you know?

With the hammerhead shark's eyes at either end of its hammer-shaped head, this shark has outstanding binocular vision and an ability to see through 360 degrees.

Human threat

Sport and commercial fishing, accidental netting, poaching, and pollution make humans a shark's number one predator.

Supreme carnivores

Hunting sharks pursue dolphins, fish, squid, seals, and turtles. Cruisers swim open-mouthed, eating whatever enters. The bottom dwellers live on crabs, clams, and molluscs.

Needle-sharp teeth of a sand tiger shark

Teeth for tearing

A hunting shark's large working teeth are at the front with rows of increasingly smaller teeth set behind. New teeth are always being grown to replace those lost. Sharks don't chew, but tear their prey and swallow great chunks. The teeth are set in skin, not bone, so teeth can move to fill a gap.

Feeding frenzy

Sharks like to dine alone, and when a number of sharks fight over the same prey a real frenzy can ensue. Sharks mass around the prey, thrashing and biting anything within reach—a behavior seen in other animals. It is thought a frenzy occurs when prey sends out distress signals.

A school of lemon sharks in a feeding frenzy

Mega feeders

Megamouths, basking sharks, and manta rays are filter feeders. A basking shark can draw up to 2,000 tons of water an hour into its mouth. The water is expelled through the gills, leaving food trapped on the denticles. The megamouth has tiny light-emitting organs around its mouth to attract small fish.

A megamouth, in full feeding mode

Fact file

An apex predator

Sharks top the food chain since they have no predators in their ecosystem. They keep in check the population of animals lower in the chain.

Great white shark

Built for speed and armed for hunting (it has 300 teeth), it is intelligent, has highly developed senses, and can live for 60 years.

Tiger shark

Found in warm, shallow coastal waters, this shark will eat anything, including sea snakes, stingrays, and trash—even car tires!

Bull shark

This is one of the most dangerous sharks. It is very strong, territorial, and unpredictable. It bumps its prey—and then eats it.

Crustaceans

Crustacea is a difficult group to **define** because it is a diverse collection of 30,000 to 45,000 species. Crustaceans **dominate** water in the same way that **insects** dominate land, although some live on land, too. Some crustaceans spend their lives **fixed** to objects, some move about **freely**. The hermit and mangrove crabs, for example, can **climb** trees! Crustaceans can't even agree on how to eat. There are **hunters**, filter feeders, scavengers, and parasites. Their size varies enormously, too. They can be so **tiny** they live between grains of sand—or **giant** like the Japanese spider crab.

Facts and figures

Largest barnacle
The giant barnacle, which is found off the coasts of Spain and Chile, grows to a foot in height.

Biggest crab
The Japanese spider crab measures 12 feet across.

Deep-sea crustacean
The tiny, prawnlike *Hirondellea gigas* lives in the Marianas Trench —almost 7 miles under the Pacific Ocean.

Smallest crab
The male pea crab measures one centimeter across.

Heavyweight
At 48 pounds, the blue-green-brown American lobster is the heaviest crustacean.

Run away!
When a shrimp moves forward, it walks. But for rapid escapes, it swims backward by curling and uncurling its abdomen.

Did you know?

The sea slater is a crustacean and is found wherever there is water. Tiny and abundant, it is critical in food chains. Some make their home on host fish as parasites.

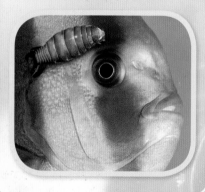

The aggressive peacock mantis shrimp strikes its prey with force (100 times its own weight) and speed (75 mph)

Hermit crab

The hermit crab is not a true crab. It has a soft underbody that it protects by making its home inside a discarded shell. As it grows, it moves into larger shells.

Pistol shrimp

One snap of the pistol shrimp's giant claw can kill its prey. It lives in colonies with a queen and worker shrimps.

As a crustacean grows, it sheds its exoskeleton to accomodate its expanding body!

To cut or crush?

The pincers, or claws, of a common lobster are different sizes. The smaller claw has sharper edges and is for cutting. The larger is used for crushing prey. A fanlike tail helps it balance. It can grow to 3 feet in length, weigh up to 11 pounds, and it can walk as well as swim.

Hungry crabs

Crabs primarily eat algae, but will also feed on molluscs, worms, bacteria, other crustaceans, and leftovers. It appears that the largest crabs are those that consume plants and animals. The chewing part of eating happens inside the stomach, which is lined with ridges for grinding the food down.

Common lobster: formidable pincers

A red rock crab scavenging on a rope

Feathery plume

The gooseneck barnacle is a filter-feeder. It has feathery tentacles that emerge from the shell to strain food out of flowing water. Highly prized as a food, gathering the barnacle takes daring. It attaches itself to rocks and other objects by a long stalk, thriving on shores that are pounded by waves.

Feathery gooseneck barnacle tentacles

Fact file

Crustacean groups

Some crustaceans are commercially valuable, and as such their stocks can be dangerously reduced by overfishing.

Krill
In the Southern Ocean their mass is 417 million tons, which is more than Earth's human mass. Krill eat plankton.

Barnacles
These filter-feeders live on any hard surface, even shelled animals. Once "glued" to a home, they build a shell for life.

Crab, shrimp, and lobster
These have a hard exoskeleton of chitin and calcium. Their multiple limbs can spear, crush, or catch prey.

Echinoderms

Sea urchins, starfish, and **crown** of thorns are among the most well-known echinoderms. They are present in all **oceans** at every depth, even in the dark **abyss** (deep sea) zone. These unusual animals have a **hydraulic** network of canals in their bodies that power tiny tube feet. All enchinoderms have radial **symmetry**. This is easiest to spot in **starfish**, as their arms extend outward from the center of their bodies in a symmetrical **pattern**. These incredible animals are able to **regenerate** missing limbs, arms, spines—even **intestines**!

Starfish range in diameter from 3/4 inch to 4 feet!

The Egyptian starfish has a protective, bony skin and can regenerate itself using part of a severed limb

Did you know?

A starfish eats a sea urchin by wrapping itself around the urchin and pushing its stomach out through its mouth. Acids dissolve the spines and shell, leaving the meat to be eaten.

Scare tactics

To alarm a predator, a sea cucumber can force its organs out through its body. Luckily, it can regrow these organs.

Sea hedgehog

Sea urchins were once called sea hedgehogs. It is easy to see the spiny similarity between urchins and hedgehogs. Long ago, in old English, urchin was the name for a hedgehog!

Tube feet

An echinoderm moves around (or sticks fast) thanks to its "feet"— thousands of tiny tubes on the animal's underside. Water is forced from sacs into the tubes to make the suckerlike feet extend or contract. The tubes also allow the animal to feed and breathe. An adult sunflower starfish has about 15,000 tube feet.

Hollow tubes end in suckerlike feet

Fact file

Heartless and brainless

Each segment of an echinoderm's body contains identical sets of internal organs. It has no heart or brain.

Sand dollars

The five-point star on the sand dollar's disclike body is covered with tiny purple spines used for movement and breathing.

Feather stars

These have 10–120 arms that branch out from five arms at the center. Grooves along each arm carry food to the mouth.

Sea cucumbers

These have wormlike bodies that can grow to 3 feet in length. Some are fairly smooth; others are bristled or bumpy.

A five-limbed red cushion starfish

A seventeen-limbed crown of thorns starfish

Natural symmetry

All echinoderms have radial symmetry, often based on the number five. This means that lines of even length can be drawn from the limbs to one central point. These animals have no left or right, only an upper side and an underside. This symmetry means than every facet of an immobile echinoderm can defend and gather food.

Hidden mouths

A sea urchin's mouth is on the urchin's underside and is surrounded by protective spines that trap food. Its mouth, like that of a starfish, has five feeding plates. The mouth of the sea cucumber is surrounded by feeding tentacles that can be retracted.

Five feeding plates in a sea urchin's mouth

Seabirds

Seabirds spend so much time away from **land**, it is difficult to comprehend their lives on the **wing**. They fly astounding **distances**, often through near-gale-force winds over angry oceans, dropping from the sky to **snatch** a fish. And all to be able to **nest** on a tiny outcrop of rock. Then, after dedicating months to raising their **young**, they set off for the hazardous return journey. Seabirds, like many other animals, are **threatened** by invasive predators at nesting sites, trash and **pollution** in the oceans, and accidental long-lining by **commercial** fishing fleets.

Facts and figures

Super migrator
Arctic terns live for up to 30 years and travel more than a million miles (equal to three round trips to the Moon) in their lifetime.

Sun filters
The retinas of a seabird's eyes contain a red-colored oil that cuts the glare reflected off sand and water.

Smallest seabird
The storm petrel is a tiny 5–10 inches.

Deep diver
The emperor penguin can dive 1,850 feet and stay underwater for 20 minutes.

Largest wing span
That belongs to the wandering albatross—at a massive 11 feet.

In danger
Of 346 seabird species, 97 are threatened, with the albatross a big concern. Nearly half of all seabird species have declining populations.

Dull but clever

A seabird's light-colored underside is hard to spot against the sky; the dull upper side veils it against the water below.

Wing shape

To aid long-distance flying, some seabirds have long, tapered wings. This improves a bird's ability to soar on currents, saving energy. Diving birds have shorter wings.

A diving gannet, with a fish firmly grasped in its beak, breaks through the water's surface

Burrow-nesting petrels
use smell to navigate to their musky nesting burrows.

Did you know?

The wandering albatross can live for over 40 years, spending 85 percent of those years at sea. It can travel 10,000 miles in a single journey and circle the globe in 46 days!

Webbed feet

Webbed feet help seabirds to paddle efficiently and propel them across the water fast enough to get liftoff. The addition of claws on webbed feet makes fishing easier. Blue feet (see right) don't help boobies swim, but will give a male a better chance of courting a female than a male with dull feet.

No mistaking blue-footed boobies

Bass Island, Scotland, hosting gannets

Back on land

Each summer, hundreds of thousands of seabirds squeeze onto rocky outcrops, small islands, and cliffs in order to nest. There is safety in numbers—predators find it hard to pick out a victim when the birds are packed tightly together. This is important since seabirds often only lay one egg.

Salty water

If you spend your life in, on, under, or over seawater, you are going to take in a lot of salt when you eat or drink. An excess would cause dehydration, which is why most seabirds have a gland that extracts the salt from their food and water. It is discharged from their nostrils.

A herring gull secreting excess salt

Glossary

Algae
A single or multi-celled organism that has no roots, stems or leaves and is often found in water.

Apex predator
An animal who has no natural predators in its ecosystem. Apex predators sit at the top of the food chains. Apex predators include whale sharks, bull sharks, killer whales, humpback whales and polar bears.

Bacteria
Microscopic living organisms, usually one-celled, that can be found everywhere.

Camouflage
Colours, patterns and shapes that make an animal difficult to see against its background.

Consumers
All animals are consumers. They are unable to make their own food, so they need to consume plants and/or animals to obtain energy.

Crustacean
An animal, such as a crab or lobster, that has a hard covering, or exoskeleton, and two pairs of antennas, or feelers.

Currents
A continuous flow of water in the ocean. Some currents are surface currents while other currents are much deeper, flowing hundreds metres below the water's surface.

Decomposers
An organism, such as a bacteria or fungus, that consumes dead organisms and returns them to ecological cycles.

Denticle
A small tooth or tooth-like projection.

Echinoderm
Marine invertebrates with tube feet and radially symmetrical bodies, such as starfish, sea urchins and sea cucumbers.

Echolocation
A method of sensing nearby objects by using pulses of high-frequency sound. Echoes bounce back from obstacles and other animals.

Ecosystem
A community of plants or animals and the environment to which they are adapted.

Equator
An imaginary line around Earth, which separates the Northern and Southern hemispheres.

Exoskeleton
An external skeleton that supports and protects an animal's body. Some exoskeletons cannot grow, so have to be shed and replaced at times during the animals life.

Filter feeders
An animal that collects food by straining small prey from seawater.

Food chain
A a community of organisms in which one forms food for another, which in turn is eaten by another, and so on.

Fungi
Organisms, such as mushrooms and moulds, that contain no chlorophyll and that live parasitically on living and dead organisms.

Gills
Organs that collect oxygen from water and are used for breathing.

Glacier
A huge mass of ice formed from snow falling and accumulating over years.

Isopod
A crustacean with seven pairs of legs adapted for crawling.

Molluscs
An animal, such as a snail or squid, with no backbone and a soft body that is often partly, or fully covered by a shell.

Overfishing
The practice of fishing so much that the fish are unable to sustain their population. The fish get fewer and fewer, until eventually there are none left to catch.

Photosynthesis
A chemical process that allows organisms to capture energy in sunlight and convert it into food.

Phytoplankton
Microscopic plants that live in the ocean and form the plant components of plankton.

Plankton
Small plant and animal organisms that float or drift in great numbers in fresh or salt water. It is the first link in the marine food chain and is eaten by many organisms, including mussels, fish, birds, and some marine mammals.

Producers
Organisms that produce their own food. They do this by converting light energy from the Sun.

Radial symmetry
A form of symmetry in which the body is shaped like a wheel, often with the mouth in the centre.

Tornado
A funnel of spinning air that forms beneath a thundercloud.

Toxins
A poison produced by certain animals, plants, or bacteria.

Waves
Waves are disturbances in the ocean that transmit energy from one place to another. Waves are usually created by wind on the ocean's surface.

Zooplankton
The tiny animal parts of plankton. Zooplankton is mainly made up of small crustaceans and the larvae of fish.

Index